LOYALTY
GOING BEYOND
FAITHFULNESS

Life Lessons from
Jonathan, King David, and Others

Parsons Publishing House
Christiansburg, Virginia USA

LOYALTY: Going Beyond Faithfulness
by Ed King

Parsons Publishing House
Christiansburg, VA 24073 USA
www.ParsonsPublishingHouse.com
Info@ParsonsPublishingHouse.com

This book or parts thereof may not be reproduced in any form, stored in a retrieval system, or transmitted in any form by any means – electronic, mechanical, photocopy, recording or otherwise—without prior written permission of the publisher, except as provided by the United States copyright law.

All Scripture quotations, unless otherwise indicated, are taken from the *Holy Bible, King James Version* (Public Domain). Scripture quotations marked (NIV) are taken from the *Holy Bible, New International Version*®, NIV®. Copyright © 1973, 1978, 1984 by Biblica, Inc.™ Used by permission of Zondervan. All rights reserved worldwide. www.zondervan.com. Scripture quotations marked (AMP) are taken from the *Amplified® Bible*. Copyright © 1954, 1958, 1962, 1964, 1965, 1987 by The Lockman Foundation. Used by permission. Scripture quotations marked (TLB) are taken from *The Living Bible* copyright © 1971. Used by permission of Tyndale House Publishers, Inc., Carol Stream, Illinois 60188. All rights reserved. Scripture quotations marked "CEV" are from the *Contemporary English Version*. Copyright © 1991, 1992, 1995 by American Bible Society, Used by Permission. Scripture taken from the *Common English Bible*®, CEB® Copyright © 2010, 2011 by Common English Bible.™ Used by permission. All rights reserved worldwide. The "CEB" and "Common English Bible" trademarks are registered in the United States Patent and Trademark Office by Common English Bible. Use of either trademark requires the permission of Common English Bible.

Copyright © 2016 by Ed King

All rights reserved.

ISBN -13: 978-1-60273-079-3
ISBN -10: 1-60273-079-2
Library of Congress Control Number: 2015918936

Printed in the United States of America.
For World-Wide Distribution.

Table of Contents

Introduction		v
1	Willingness to Change	1
2	Evidence for Faithfulness	5
3	Exploring Faithfulness	11
4	The Blessings of Faithfulness	19
5	Journey Into Loyalty	21
6	Covenant of Loyalty	27
7	Loyalty is Greater Than Blood	37
8	Beyond Faithfulness Into Loyalty	43
9	What Does Loyalty Look Like?	49
10	What Does Loyalty Say?	55
11	Loyalty Goes the Extra Mile	61
12	A Holy Covenant	69
13	Protecting Loyalties	77
14	Faithfulness vs. Loyalty	91
About the Author		95

LOYALTY: GOING BEYOND FAITHFULNESS

Introduction

One truth or idea alone does not build a solid, capable Christian. In fact, it takes a great deal more than that to build an effective life for Christ. The introduction of a new and accurate concept or simply the right word at the right time can be essential in challenging the way a person thinks about a subject. That word or concept can certainly help change their direction toward the vitally important path that God wants them to take.

Although the subject of loyalty may not seem to be extremely exciting to you on the surface, it is, without question, critically important and revolutionary. If you will give this truth proper attention and regard it properly, it may be just the impetus needed to propel

LOYALTY: GOING BEYOND FAITHFULNESS

you into a much deeper and fulfilling relationship with the Lord. All of us are on a journey with our ultimate destination being heaven, but there is much to do between here and there.

Tests come to us all, but when wise people face a challenge, they respond to it in a positive way, and it causes them to take new steps in the Lord. Foolish people are prone to do just the opposite. They tend to ignore or run from challenges. Finding challenges too difficult and oppressive, they tend to ignore or run from them. The Bible says that you cannot rebuke a fool; they won't listen.

> If you rebuke a mocker, you will only get a smart retort; yes, he will snarl at you. So don't bother with him; he will only hate you for trying to help him. But a wise man, when rebuked, will love you all the more (Proverbs 9:7-8, TLB).

This book does not contain a message of rebuke, but one of encouragement: a victory message! My hope is that while we are on this journey into a new area of truth, you will allow the Spirit of God to broaden your mind to think in ways you possibly have not considered before.

Your decision to take this step in the Lord into loyalty will be a good one. However, if you decide not to take this step, regardless of the reason, the possibility exists that a year from today the same struggles will still be troubling you. The same problems, the same battles—

Introduction

circumnavigating the same mountain in the same wilderness—will still be there, and you will still be complaining about the very same conditions that may be prevalent in your life today.

In other words, if you continue to live your life the way you always have, you will remain exactly the way you are. You will never make progress. It's time for your next step. Take it!

Dr. Ed King
Knoxville, Tennessee

LOYALTY: GOING BEYOND FAITHFULNESS

CHAPTER 1
Willingness to Change

"Most men will proclaim every one his own goodness; but a faithful man who can find?" (Proverbs 20:6).

Motivation is something that comes from within. As a pastor, you can do all the motivational speaking you desire to, but it is not going to accomplish anything in and of itself. There must be something inside the hearer—a desire to change circumstances or take steps to improve themselves—that causes them to respond in a particular way.

I have preached in venues where people sat with their arms folded across their collective chests daring me to inspire them. The problem is that when people make

LOYALTY: GOING BEYOND FAITHFULNESS

the decision to reject inspiration under any circumstance, they will be overwhelmingly successful at stopping it. There will be no transference of motivation for them. The truth is that you can't motivate people beyond their willingness to be motivated. You cannot launch an unwilling person into action. Action is a decision, and they must first decide to take action inside themselves. The initiative must start deep within them.

The Bible says in the book of Titus, "A man that is an heretick after the first and second admonition reject" (Titus 3:10). When we look at it from the Living Bible, it becomes clearer.

> If anyone is causing divisions among you, he should be given a first and second warning. After that have nothing more to do with him (Titus 3:10, TLB).

You can only deal with a divisive person like that up to a point. You are eventually going to have to tell them that they must become responsible for themselves, take charge of their actions, and correct their faulty behavior.

You may have been well-taught, but if you do not do anything with the information you have learned, it's not going to do you any good. I do not believe, however, that if you have simply been lazy or unmotivated that you are destined to remain that way. Laziness is truly a contagious disease, but you do not have to catch it. With God's help, you can do something positive about it—take action to the contrary and refuse to have anything resembling laziness become a part of you. Train yourself to become a person of faithfulness, diligence, and hard work.

God is Faithful

The Bible speaks about the subject of faithfulness in various places. It says in Galatians, "But the fruit of the Spirit is love, joy, peace, forbearance, kindness, goodness, faithfulness, gentleness and self-control" (Galatians 5:22-23, NIV). This passage tells us that faithfulness is a fruit of the Spirit which conveys the character of God in and to us.

God is faithful. For this reason, when He comes into our lives in the person of the Holy Spirit, we exemplify the faithfulness He shows to us. The Bible tells us that God is as faithful as the sunrise, and every morning we can get up and have the confidence to believe that another day will begin. We have that assurance. King Solomon expounds on God's faithfulness:

> His name shall endure for ever: his name shall be continued as long as the sun: and men shall be blessed in him: all nations shall call him blessed (Psalm 72:17).

Relationships necessitate faithfulness as well. You cannot be unfaithful to your friends and expect to remain in good standing with them. The fact is, you are most likely going to lose them. Additionally, it is impossible to have both a wholesome and unfaithful marriage at the same time. Faithfulness directly relates to the word "fidelity." Therefore, an unfaithful person and an infidel are synonymous; they fit together hand-in-glove.

Faithfulness is a quality that comes from God; we as Christians should do our best to demonstrate, emulate, operate, and practice faithfulness in our lives.

CHAPTER 2

Evidence for Faithfulness

> And we have sent with them our brother, whom we have oftentimes proved diligent in many things, but now much more diligent, upon the great confidence which I have in you (2 Corinthians 8:22).

The Bible says that faithfulness must be proven. It also tells us that we need to attest to the character of people who work in certain positions in the church or the ministry. Some might say, "You should believe in me because I'm here; I show up. I'm here every Sunday and Wednesday night of the year. There's nobody more dedicated than I am." That really may seem like a valid argument on the surface, but it is simply not good enough. It's too shallow.

For example, what if a convicted child molester unknown to you, signed up to work in your children's department? They may be faithful in their attendance, but their motivation is perverted. If you fail in your due diligence to determine that person's background, then how will you ever know the truth? It is the responsibility of those in charge to look into people's character for the express purpose of proving them. You will need to do that in your life and relationships, too.

We need to do a little "reference checking" in the body of Christ. Just because a person is willing does not mean they are able. A person may desire greatly to take part in a ministry or activity, but they may not be found trustworthy or faithful to participate.

Being Found Faithful

> "Moreover it is required in stewards
> that a man be found faithful"
> (1 Corinthians 4:2).

The word "found" indicates a search is involved. You don't find something unless you are looking for it. You might stumble upon it quite by accident, but a "find" is something that is unidentified—concealed, unknown, or unrevealed—until discovered.

Some discoveries make you happy, and some do not, but it's still a "find." With kids in your house, I promise you, you find things—all kinds of things—some of which you wish you hadn't. When you remove the cushions from the couch and dig down into those large, dark, crevices, there's no way in the world to know what's lurking down there. It's a little unsettling. You might find forty-seven crayons, six ink pens, three half-eaten cookies, or a cheese sandwich from six months ago. You might even find enough money to send your kids to college! Finding money in any amount makes you happy; finding a six-month-old cheese sandwich...not so much!

So the Bible says a steward must be found faithful. That means you have to watch that person carefully to see if there is that quality of faithfulness in them. It may be well-hidden or undeveloped, so you have to be diligent to find it.

Faithfulness Above Ability

Paul spoke to Timothy concerning the concept of faithfulness over ability. In Second Timothy he says:

> And the things that thou hast heard of me among many witnesses, the same commit thou to faithful men who shall be able to teach others also (2 Timothy 2:2).

Faithfulness is more important than a person's ability. You should hire hearts, not heads. A person with incredible skills and an unfaithful heart will do you more harm than good every time. A faithful or loyal person with great abilities is the one you're after. Faithfulness is entry level and mandatory, in the service of God, and it cannot be bypassed or ignored. Faithfulness is a positive quality, and must be present, but we must also go beyond it. Faithfulness comes before loyalty.

The Proof of Time

One of the best ways to prove faithfulness is with time. If you would merely assign a few small responsibilities to people—just a little at a time—you will certainly discover how faithful they are.

In the world of business, there is a well-known concept called "The Peter Principle." It's a humorous, but valid principle that says, "A person will only rise to the level of their incompetence." A few years ago, a survey among the CEOs (Chief Executive Officers) of some major corporations seemed to prove "The Peter Principle" correct. After analyzing the surveys, the results indicated that two-out-of-ten of these specific top executives surveyed would be terminated within a year. The survey proved true.

The reason? The executives ceased to grow and contribute to the success of their organization. They had risen to the level of their satisfaction that became the level of their incompetence. Their motivation ceased or waned considerably, and, as a result, they became of no real value to their company.

Growth in the Kingdom

The kingdom of God is similar to the business environment because we are all involved in a growth process—each of us rising to the level of our incompetence. We, too, must accept the challenge to develop, progress, and improve.

Self-improvement means that you must make demands of yourself. Self-improvement forces you to learn new things and necessitates the implementation of them. You may have been of great value to an organization in its infancy, but if you do not grow along with it, your value will be lost.

The church is no different. You can set your own promotion in motion there as well. It is crucial for you to be a person who can recognize the signs of the times, change with them, and move positively ahead in God.

Winning the Game of Life

If you heed my advice without allowing your pride to get in the way, I can show you how to win at this so-called "game of life." Life, however, is not a game at all, but serious business. None of us knows everything, and we all need help from time to time. Don't sabotage your progress by getting your feelings hurt or your "feathers ruffled."

I am both a pastor and an employer. I have had more than forty employees at one given time working in the church I pastor, and I have gained personal knowledge concerning principles of business and the kingdom of God. The truth is, there isn't a single leader who becomes successful in these positions by being foolish or lucky. You have to know what you are doing and be confident in your abilities.

LOYALTY: GOING BEYOND FAITHFULNESS

CHAPTER 3
Exploring Faithfulness

Through the Bible, God gives us categories of faithfulness. For example, He said in the sixteenth chapter of Luke, that if you were faithful with the little things, He would make you a ruler or caretaker, over the considerably larger things—the more important things.

> He that is faithful in that which is least is faithful also in much: and he that is unjust in the least is unjust also in much (Luke 16:10).

God said that if you are faithful with unrighteous mammon or money, He would not have a problem trusting you with His true riches—the spiritual riches of the kingdom. We see this when Luke quotes Jesus, "If therefore ye have not been faithful in the unrighteous mammon, who will commit to your trust the true riches?" (Luke 16:11).

God looks at those areas in your life—not just once, but many times—to see how you are accomplishing the things entrusted to you. If you are not faithful with someone else's material goods, God will not give you your own. Jesus teaches, "And if ye have not been faithful in that which is another man's, who shall give you that which is your own?" (Luke 16:12). God will continually test you to see just how dependable and trustworthy you really are.

You will never be a good employer unless you are first a good employee. You will never be a person who can command authority unless you first become a servant. These are characteristics of how the kingdom works, and it is God who sets these principles of faithfulness in motion.

Faithfulness is Unchanging

If you are going to be a faithful person, you must first be a person of your word. In Psalm fifteen King David wrote, "He that sweareth to his own hurt, and changeth not" (Psalms 15:4) which means that when a faithful man makes a promise, he keeps it no matter what. We can see this more clearly in The Contemporary English Version of the Bible which makes it a little more understandable, "And they keep their promises, no matter what the cost" (Psalms 15:4, CEV).

Just like you, I have given my word, promising to do things—some of those things were major purchases—but upon further consideration, I wished I could have reversed my decision. For example, have you noticed how wonderful that new car looks until you have made five or six payments on it? Even that new car smell doesn't do it for you anymore. It doesn't matter; you're still locked into your contract. The lender is not going to let you out of your contract just because you're not quite as enamored with it anymore.

You may argue, "Well, I don't like it. I think I'll just let it go back." Really? Even to consider defaulting on a loan shows something intrinsically flawed in your character. If you even think in those terms, it's a characteristic likened to an unfaithful person. The Living Bible translation says, "Evil men borrow and cannot pay it back! But the good man returns what he owes with some extra besides" (Psalm 37:21, TLB).

Remember, you created the debt, not the lender. They offered the goods or services for sale, and enticed you—sometimes unmercifully—by using many effective marketing techniques, but you signed the note! There were no family members taken hostage or guns aimed at your head. You made a conscious decision to buy whatever it was and signed the note.

Keeping Commitments

A faithful person works even when it's difficult and even when they don't feel well. You need to be faithful even when you absolutely don't want to be where you're supposed to be. Your flesh may want to be out on the golf course instead of teaching ten-year-old boys about Jesus. As tempting as that may be, you still need to be faithful. Piece of advice: leave the clubs in the trunk and keep your commitments.

Have you ever felt like you had to go somewhere that you knew God wanted you, but nothing inside of you wanted to go? After trying every way imaginable to get out of the commitment, it still went on the calendar. Even after telling the Lord that you really didn't want to go, you went anyway. People were waiting for you there, and they needed what God had placed on the inside of you.

In the book of Psalms the Bible says, "O love the Lord, all ye his saints: for the Lord preserveth the faithful, and plentifully rewardeth the proud doer" (Psalms 31:23). What a great promise to us from God: He said that if we are faithful, He would preserve us! The Common English Version of the Bible says it this way:

> All you who are faithful, love the Lord! The Lord protects those who are loyal, but he pays the proud back to the fullest degree (Psalms 31:23, CEB).

The Perfect Way

> Mine eyes shall be upon the faithful of the land, that they may dwell with me: he that walketh in a perfect way, he shall serve me (Psalms 101:6).

God called faithfulness the "perfect way." He said that faithfulness is a characteristic that takes us into the very presence or dwelling of God Himself!

We also see in Psalms where God said that He would bless the children of the faithful. That's just like God, isn't it? He is not only going to bless you for being faithful, but He is also going to bless your children and their children as well!

> But the loving-kindness of the Lord is from everlasting to everlasting to those who reverence him; his salvation is to children's children of those who are faithful to his covenant and remember to obey him! (Psalms 103:17-18).

The subject of faithfulness is an important topic, and many Scriptures deal with it. A verse in Proverbs says, "Drink from your own well, my son—be faithful and true to your wife" (Proverbs 5:15, TLB). God requires faithfulness in marriage. You are certainly a wise person if you are faithful and true to your spouse.

Characteristics of Faithfulness

There are several characteristics that all faithful people have in common:

- A faithful person controls their tongue.

It's a wise person who knows when to speak, and when to keep his mouth closed. Scripture tells us, "A talebearer revealeth secrets; but he that is of a faithful spirit concealeth the matter" (Proverbs 11:13).

LOYALTY: GOING BEYOND FAITHFULNESS

- A faithful person operates with discretion.

God says that people who gossip are unfaithful, but a person who refrains from revealing another person's sins, problems, or indiscretions is a faithful person. God does not want you going from one person to another spreading idle gossip. The Bible says, "A gossip tells everything, but a true friend will keep a secret" (Proverbs 11:13, CEV).

- A faithful person has the propensity to cover for another. Love covers; it doesn't reveal. As a Christian, that is the way we should strive to live because it's the right thing to do.

- A faithful person brings life, not death.
> "A wicked messenger falleth into mischief;
> but a faithful ambassador is health"
> (Proverbs 13:17).

- A faithful person tells the truth.
> "A faithful witness will not lie; but a
> false witness will utter lies"
> (Proverbs 14:5).

That includes even those in the pulpit! I've heard stories from the pulpit that bother me—things we preachers say, exaggerations we make, half-truths we tell that go too far—when using words that make us look good while conveniently ignoring our flaws.

- Faithful people are good employees.

God says that an employee is to be faithful to his or her employer. If you are taking their money as wages, be faithful to them. Do not talk negatively about them, saying things like, "I hate this job." You don't hate it enough to stop cashing your paycheck, do you?

- Faithful people are energizing.
    "A faithful employee is as refreshing as a
    cool day in the hot summertime"
    (Proverbs 25:13, TLB).

True Love is Faithful

"Faithful are the wounds of a friend, but the
kisses of an enemy are deceitful"
(Proverbs 27:6).

A person who genuinely loves you is a person you can rely on to be faithful in all aspects of their relationship with you. They may even need to tell you something that is hard for you to hear, but it would be for your own good. Initially, it may upset, hurt, or offend you, but they will say it with more love than a deceitful person would when they falsely flatter you for self-serving reasons.

I have found over the process of time that usually the more a person tells me he loves me and flatters me, the less faithful he proves to be. When I hear "Oh, Pastor, I'd never hurt you. I love you; you're great," I count it as a warning. Usually, such a person proves to be a problem.

I remember one man, in particular, who reassured me repeatedly of how loyal and faithful he was. However, in my entire life on this planet, I have never met a more unfaithful and deceitful person based on all the falsehearted things he did. I think he was telling me those stories to convince himself of his faithfulness. I think he knew in his heart all along that he was a disloyal and unfaithful person, but he wanted to convince himself that he wasn't.

To paraphrase Queen Gertrude in Shakespeare's Hamlet, "The [gentleman] doth protest too much, methinks." In other words, the more you try to convince someone of your sincere motives, the more suspect your sincerity can become. The more you verbally assert your faithfulness, sincerity, or loyalty toward a person or thing, chances are you are probably trying to convince yourself and them that you are someone that you're really not.

CHAPTER 4
The Blessings of Faithfulness

"A faithful man shall abound with blessings; but he that maketh haste to be rich shall not be innocent" (Proverbs 28:20).

The Bible says that faithfulness will cause us to abound with blessings. You can see from the Scripture that faithfulness is something God says He absolutely requires.

Paul emphasized faithfulness in his letters to Timothy. First, he said God recognized his faithfulness, "I thank Christ Jesus our Lord, who hath enabled me, for that he counted me faithful, putting me into the ministry" (1 Timothy 1:12). Paul also said that ministers should be faithful:

LOYALTY: GOING BEYOND FAITHFULNESS

> And the things that thou hast heard of me among many witnesses, the same commit thou to faithful men who shall be able to teach others also (2 Timothy 2:2).

God said that the gospel is entrusted to faithful people. We grant certain responsibilities and authority in the church based on an individual's faithfulness. However, if a person does not prove to be faithful, that person should not be given responsibilities and authority, else negative consequences will most likely result.

Have you ever put confidence in someone who did not produce? The Bible says, "Confidence in an unfaithful man in time of trouble is like a broken tooth, and a foot out of joint" (Proverbs 25:19). Now think about the last severe toothache you had or imagine how painful it would be to have a disjointed foot and that's what it feels like to trust someone who is not faithful. It would be a terrible burden on you to accomplish anything while suffering from those conditions. Everyday activities that should be second nature—routine activities such as eating, drinking, and walking—would become extremely challenging.

Faithfulness is a wonderful quality, but faithfulness can be mechanical, too. You can learn to be a faithful person. You can do the right things. You can take the right actions. You can move into gear. You can become a faithful person simply because you want to. In fact, I believe you can become anything you want to be if you want it badly enough. When you decide to be faithful, blessings will follow.

CHAPTER 5

Journey Into Loyalty

Faithfulness is a great starting place, but it is definitely not the end of our journey. We are now going to go beyond faithfulness and continue our quest for knowledge out into deeper water exploring the subject of loyalty.

There is a distinct difference between the characteristics of faithfulness and loyalty. A person can be faithful, but not necessarily loyal. Faithfulness is a learned response that often comes from the head. Loyalty, on the other hand, comes from the heart and is felt much more deeply.

Loyalty has been and should be the cry of the moment, not just in the local church, but in the entire body of

Christ. The subject I'm going to share with you now will change you considerably if you will take it to heart and allow it to penetrate your spirit. It will revolutionize your life.

The Minimum Requirement

Let's begin by looking at 1 Samuel:

> And it came to pass, when he had made an end of speaking unto Saul, that the soul of Jonathan was knit with the soul of David, and Jonathan loved him as his own soul. And Saul took him that day, and would let him go no more home to his father's house. Then Jonathan and David made a covenant, because he loved him as his own soul. And Jonathan stripped himself of the robe that was upon him, and gave it to David, and his garments, even to his sword, and to his bow, and to his girdle (1 Samuel 18:1-4).

The concept I want you to see is something that is called, for lack of a better term, a "soul tie" or "soulmate." The Bible says that the souls of Jonathan and David were "knit" together. They truly knew one another. They almost knew what the other would say or do before they said or did anything.

Conversely, we have also experienced being in a large room with many people present but have absolutely no soul-tie or harmony of heart with any of them. We might know them all, but feel no responsibility or kinship with any.

Similarly, we can be mechanically faithful to our employer without having any loyalty whatsoever to them. We may do what we are asked to do and be there when he says to be there, but we may not care at all about his personal success or that of his business. If that's you, you're faithful, but not loyal.

The church functions that way today. We have a plethora of faithful people, but God is looking for something deeper. He is looking for loyal people.

Faithfulness is fundamental. The Bible says, "Moreover it is required in stewards that a man be found faithful" (1 Corinthians 4:2). It's entry-level service. Faithfulness is the beginning—not where you should be aspiring to finish. Some people have taken faithfulness to be their destination, but God says faithfulness is the minimum requirement. When you're faithful you haven't arrived; you have only started.

Loyal Brothers: David & Jonathan

David and Jonathan's hearts were knit together as tightly as an expensive wool sweater. They became more than faithful companions and more than co-workers. They became loyal brothers in the Lord, committed to one another.

After Jonathan died, King David honored his covenant with Jonathan by honoring Mephibosheth, Jonathan's son. Other people also came to David after he was king, but David remembered his covenant with Jonathan and gave Mephibosheth a preferred position.

David was faithful to all people in his kingdom, but he was not loyal to all of them. He was, however, loyal to Jonathan's family, and ultimately to Jonathan's son Mephibosheth.

> One day David began wondering if any of Saul's family was still living, for he wanted to be kind to them, as he had promised Prince Jonathan. He heard about a man named Ziba, who had been one of Saul's servants, and summoned him. "Are you Ziba?" the king asked. "Yes, sir, I am," he replied. The king then asked him, "Is anyone left from Saul's family? If so, I want to fulfill a sacred vow by being kind to him." "Yes," Ziba replied, "Jonathan's lame son is still alive." "Where is he?" the king asked. "In Lo-debar," Ziba told him. "At the home of Machir." So King David sent for Mephibosheth—Jonathan's son and Saul's grandson. Mephibosheth arrived in great fear and greeted the king in deep humility, bowing low before him. But David said, "Don't be afraid! I've asked you to come so that I can be kind to you because of my vow to your father Jonathan. I will restore to you all the land of your grandfather Saul, and you shall live here at the palace!" Mephibosheth fell to the

ground before the king. "Should the king show kindness to a dead dog like me?" he exclaimed. Then the king summoned Saul's servant Ziba. "I have given your master's grandson everything that belonged to Saul and his family," he said. "You and your sons and servants are to farm the land for him, to produce food for his family; but he will live here with me." Ziba, who had fifteen sons and twenty servants, replied, "Sir, I will do all you have commanded." And from that time on, Mephibosheth ate regularly with King David, as though he were one of his own sons. Mephibosheth had a young son, Mica. All the household of Ziba became Mephibosheth's servants, but Mephibosheth (who was lame in both feet) moved to Jerusalem to live at the palace (2 Samuel 9:1-13, TLB).

LOYALTY: GOING BEYOND FAITHFULNESS

CHAPTER 6

Covenant of Loyalty

You cannot be loyal to everyone—faithful, yes, but not loyal. To be loyal to everyone is in all actuality, to be disloyal to everyone because it causes conflict. For example, I cannot be loyal to someone who gossips about one of my trusted friends. How could I do that? If I did, I would be totally disloyal to my friend.

God wants us to go beyond faithfulness and onward into loyalty. Becoming loyal is the requirement—even the demand—which the Holy Spirit is making on the lives of people today. What we have done in the past is not going to be acceptable in the future. If you want to take your next step in the Lord, you must settle this issue of loyalty.

LOYALTY: GOING BEYOND FAITHFULNESS

Required to be Faithful

I am required to be faithful to the body of Christ, but I cannot be loyal to every church. I can be faithful to every pastor to whom God has appointed, but I can only be loyal to one. That statement may make you uncomfortable, but we can't avoid it. If you don't walk in loyalty, you will not make any definitive progress in life. I realize it's not a popular subject, but that doesn't change anything. Let's allow God to stretch us in this area as we choose to embrace loyalty as a core characteristic of our Christian walk. Why? Because there are requirements that God has put into our lives as precursors to our next level of growth and progress in Him. There is no growth without stretching.

David and Jonathan's heart and soul were closely knit together. They had a heart-tie, which means their relationship was deeper than merely relying on being physically present with one another. We see in the Bible that David and Jonathan made a covenant. That sounds similar to a New Testament arrangement. Wouldn't you agree?

A Covenant with the Body

Some may say, "Pastor, I didn't enter into covenant with the body of Christ." I would respectfully disagree with you. The concept of communion relates to the word "community." If you haven't committed to the community, you aren't in communion. Simply put, if you don't commit to the community—the community of the body of Christ—you are not in communion with the Lord.

Covenant of Loyalty

> Who is weak, and I am not weak? who is offended, and I burn not? If I must needs glory, I will glory of the things which concern mine infirmities (2 Corinthians 11:29-30).

It's easier to see what this means by looking at The Living Bible.

> Who makes a mistake and I do not feel his sadness? Who falls without my longing to help him? Who is spiritually hurt without my fury rising against the one who hurt him? But if I must brag, I would rather brag about the things that show how weak I am (2 Corinthians 11:29-30, TLB).

We must discern the Lord's body—His church. How can you say you have honored God when you have not treated your brothers in Christ with the same honor and respect?

> And the King shall answer and say unto them, Verily I say unto you, Inasmuch as ye have done it unto one of the least of these my brethren, ye have done it unto me (Matthew 25:40).

God watches us to see how we view and treat others. He is looking for faithfulness in entry-level Christianity at every stage of service. That's how our Christian life begins: by being faithful.

LOYALTY: GOING BEYOND FAITHFULNESS

The Lord wants us to go beyond faithfulness, however, and become loyal individuals. He wants us to become people with a committed heart—a heart of integrity. God deals with us out of His integrity, and He expects us to deal with Him and others out of our integrity. The Bible says, "So he fed them according to the integrity of his heart; and guided them by the skillfulness of his hands" (Psalm 78:72).

Your ability to enter into this covenant—into this concept of loyal relationships—is determined by your integrity more so than anything else. If you do not have integrity, you cannot be truthful, and, therefore, cannot honor the covenant. If you have no integrity—no congruity or harmony of soul—how can you be loyal? The Word warns us, "A double minded man is unstable in all his ways" (James 1:8). If we don't walk with integrity all the time, we are unsteady and unpredictable.

Loyal to the Anointing

Let's look in the book of First Samuel where we find Saul telling his son, Jonathan to do something outrageous, "And Saul spake to Jonathan his son, and to all his servants, that they should kill David" (1 Samuel 19:1).

Here is the short story: Jonathan was King Saul's son. King Saul offended the Lord, and, as a result of his own actions, would not remain king. God told Samuel that the next king would come from the house of Jesse, David's father. Samuel considered all of Jesse's sons until he saw David and, by God's direction, anointed him to be king.

> The Lord said to Samuel, "How long will you mourn for Saul, since I have rejected him as king over Israel? Fill your horn with oil and be on your way; I am sending you to Jesse of Bethlehem. I have chosen one of his sons to be king." But Samuel said, "How can I go? If Saul hears about it, he will kill me." The Lord said, "Take a heifer with you and say, 'I have come to sacrifice to the Lord.' Invite Jesse to the sacrifice, and I will show you what to do. You are to anoint for me the one I indicate." Samuel did what the Lord said. When he arrived at Bethlehem, the elders of the town trembled when they met him. They asked, "Do you come in peace?" Samuel replied, "Yes, in peace; I have come to sacrifice to the Lord. Consecrate yourselves and come to the sacrifice with me." Then he consecrated Jesse and his sons and invited them to the sacrifice. When they arrived, Samuel saw Eliab and thought, "Surely the Lord's anointed stands here before the Lord." But the Lord said to Samuel, "Do not consider his appearance or his height, for I have rejected him. The Lord does not look at the things people look at. People look at the outward appearance, but the Lord looks at the heart." Then Jesse called Abinadab and had him pass in front of Samuel. But

> Samuel said, "The Lord has not chosen this one either." Jesse then had Shammah pass by, but Samuel said, "Nor has the Lord chosen this one." Jesse had seven of his sons pass before Samuel, but Samuel said to him, "The Lord has not chosen these." So he asked Jesse, "Are these all the sons you have?" "There is still the youngest," Jesse answered. "He is tending the sheep." Samuel said, "Send for him; we will not sit down until he arrives." So he sent for him and had him brought in. He was glowing with health and had a fine appearance and handsome features. Then the Lord said, "Rise and anoint him; this is the one." So Samuel took the horn of oil and anointed him in the presence of his brothers, and from that day on the Spirit of the Lord came powerfully upon David (1 Samuel 16:1-13, NIV).

Although Samuel anointed David to be king, certain events had to happen to establish his transition to the throne. David didn't immediately pack up his belongings and set off to the palace. First, there was a progression of events arranged by the hand of the Lord to give David favor in the eyes of the people of Israel which began with the slaying of Goliath, the giant.

David Slays Goliath

> Then Goliath, a Philistine champion from Gath, came out of the Philistine ranks to

face the forces of Israel. He was a giant of a man, measuring over nine feet tall! He wore a bronze helmet, a two-hundred-pound coat of mail, bronze leggings, and carried a bronze javelin several inches thick, tipped with a twenty-five-pound iron spearhead, and his armor bearer walked ahead of him with a huge shield. I defy the armies of Israel! Send me a man who will fight with me!" "Don't worry about a thing," David told him [Saul]. "I'll take care of this Philistine!" But David persisted. "When I am taking care of my father's sheep," he said, "and a lion or a bear comes and grabs a lamb from the flock, I go after it with a club and take the lamb from its mouth. If it turns on me, I catch it by the jaw and club it to death. I have done this to both lions and bears, and I'll do it to this heathen Philistine too, for he has defied the armies of the living God! The Lord who saved me from the claws and teeth of the lion and the bear will save me from this Philistine!" Saul finally consented, "All right, go ahead," he said, "and may the Lord be with you!" Then he picked up five smooth stones from a stream and put them in his shepherd's bag and, armed only with his shepherd's staff and sling, started across to Goliath. "Am I a dog," he roared at David, "that you come at me with a stick?" And he cursed David by the names of his gods. David shouted in reply, "You come to me with a sword and a spear, but I come to you in the name of the Lord of the armies of heaven and of Israel—the very God whom you have defied. Today the Lord will conquer you, and I will kill you and cut off your head; and then I will give the dead bodies of your men to the birds and wild animals, and the whole world will know that there is a God in Israel! And Israel will learn that the Lord does not depend on weapons to fulfill his plans—he works without regard to human means! He will give you to us!" As Goliath approached, David ran out to meet him and, reaching into his shepherd's bag, took out a stone, hurled it from his sling, and hit the Philistine in the forehead. The stone sank in, and the man fell on his face to the ground. So David conquered the Philistine giant with a sling and a stone. Since he had no sword, he ran over and pulled Goliath's from its sheath and killed him with it, and then cut off his head. When the Philistines saw that their champion was dead, they turned and ran (1 Samuel 17:4-7, 10, 32, 34-37, 40, 43, 45-51, TLB).

Saul knew the Spirit of the Lord had departed from him. He knew that God had taken his kingdom; the spiritual impetus or motivation behind his reign was gone even though he still physically held the title. The anointing to govern—the anointing to be king—had departed from Saul. Scripture records, "But the Spirit of the Lord departed from Saul..." (1 Samuel 16:14).

Saul became fiercely jealous as he saw the anointing come upon David. His envy and anger escalated to a fevered pitch, even to the point of wanting to kill David. However, Jonathan, Saul's son, had made a covenant with David at great risk and personal expense. Let's read on in the book of Samuel:

> And it came to pass, when he had made an end of speaking unto Saul, that the soul of Jonathan was knit with the soul of David, and Jonathan loved him as his own soul. And Saul took him that day, and would let him go no more home to his father's house. Then Jonathan and David made a covenant, because he loved him as his own soul. And Jonathan stripped himself of the robe that was upon him, and gave it to David, and his garments, even to his sword, and to his bow, and to his girdle (1 Samuel 18:1-4).

Under normal circumstances, Saul's son Jonathan would be next in line to become king. However, Jonathan recognized the anointing that God placed on David through Samuel and was willing to give away his inheritance in favor of the will of God. Just think about what Jonathan gave up. Could we do that? Could we give up our right to be king? It certainly would not be easy. Sometimes, we want to hold, control, and manipulate our circumstances. We are often afraid to surrender ourselves to the will of God because we are afraid of possible loss or the unknown. However, it is never a loss to follow God. It's the answer!

LOYALTY: GOING BEYOND FAITHFULNESS

CHAPTER 7

Loyalty is Greater Than Blood

Jonathan sincerely loved and revered David. He even went so far as to warn David that his father, Saul, was prepared to kill him.

> And Saul spake to Jonathan his son, and to all his servants, that they should kill David. But Jonathan Saul's son delighted much in David: and Jonathan told David, saying, Saul my father seeketh to kill thee: now therefore, I pray thee, take heed to thyself until the morning, and abide in a secret place, and hide thyself: And I will go out and stand beside my father in the field where thou art, and I will commune with my father of thee; and what I see, that I will tell thee (1 Samuel 19:1-3).

Jonathan's faithfulness to David was without question. However, over and above his faithfulness to him, his deep-felt loyalty moved Jonathan to take a significant risk and warn David of Saul's plot to kill him. Loyalty is a protector. Loyalty does not become a contributor to someone's downfall or failure; loyalty becomes their protector and guardian.

Family Loyalty vs. Kingdom Loyalty

Jonathan held his covenant bond with his close friend, David, in higher regard than he did his relationship with his father. Some may say, "I think that's just wrong. I don't think we should ever favor our friends above our family." My short answer to you is that you should definitely protect your godly friends if your family member or members in question are out of the will of God. That is a different story altogether. Never follow your family into a ditch, figuratively speaking. Never follow your family to your destruction. Never.

There is no loyalty involved in following your alcoholic father or your drug-addled mother who are hell-bent on ruining their lives and the lives of their family. Following a mother or father who are determined not to serve God is never more important than following a God-loving pastor or Christian leader who tells you the unvarnished truth and advises you spiritually concerning the direction of your life.

Who do you think God is? Jesus Himself could not walk with His earthly family because they didn't believe in Him! Yes, they came to a point of believing later; but early in His ministry, He had to step out into the will of God at the expense of His family relationships. Jesus' earthly family thought He had lost His mind. Mark records this observation, "When his family heard about this, they went to take charge of him, for they said, 'He is out of his mind'" (Mark 3:21, NIV).

It's not smart to think that family loyalty is more important than loyalty to the Lord and His Word. If you believe that, you're mistaken.

Some might say, "I go to church because my parents did." That's great, but you need to make spiritual decisions based on the place God occupies in your life—not the significance He holds in your parent's life. If you can go to church together, praise God for it. There's no one here telling you to be disloyal to your family; we are teaching you where loyalty actually resides. It resides in the kingdom more than it resides in being "mama called and daddy sent."

Do the Right Thing

Be God's man or woman. Have courage and some "guts" about you. Do the right thing even if your parents or family don't agree. You might say, "But my mom is my confidant." Your mother may actually be your downfall—the ticket to your destruction.

You need to have enough spiritual sense to stand up on your own two feet and make some quality kingdom decisions for yourself. When you stand before the

Lord, He is not going to ask if you did what your parents told you to do. He is going to ask if you did what He told you to do.

> There came then his brethren and his mother, and, standing without, sent unto him, calling him. And the multitude sat about him, and they said unto him, Behold, thy mother and thy brethren without seek for thee. And he answered them, saying, Who is my mother, or my brethren? And he looked round about on them which sat about him, and said, Behold my mother and my brethren! For whosoever shall do the will of God, the same is my brother, and my sister, and mother (Mark 3:31-35).

Hate Your Mom and Dad?

The Bible says you can't even follow Jesus unless you "hate" your father and mother.

> If any man come to me, and hate not his father, and mother, and wife, and children, and brethren, and sisters, yea, and his own life also, he cannot be my disciple (Luke 14:26).

Don't get all excited, the word "hate" in this context means "to love less." You must love your father and mother less than you love Jesus. Here's that verse from The Living Bible.

Loyalty is Greater Than Blood

> Anyone who wants to be my follower must love me far more than he does[a] his own father, mother, wife, children, brothers, or sisters—yes, more than his own life—otherwise he cannot be my disciple (Luke 14:26, TLB).

You must determine to follow the will of God no matter what it costs you. It doesn't matter who likes it or who doesn't.

LOYALTY: GOING BEYOND FAITHFULNESS

CHAPTER 8
Beyond Faithfulness Into Loyalty

How many times have you heard, "If it was good enough for mom and dad, it's good enough for me?" It may sound good, it may even sound accurate, but there's a problem; it is simply not true. You see, times and experiences change. Depending on your parents or grandparent's age, the whole movement of the Spirit of God quite possibly was not even in existence in their day.

If I had been preaching many years ago when John Knox was preaching, I would have probably been quite similar to him. If I had been preaching when Charles G. Finney was preaching, I would have probably been quite similar to him, as well. Similarly, I would probably have been a Methodist if I had lived in the days of John and Charles Wesley.

But we're not living in their day are we? We are not putting new wine into old wineskins. We're living in the "now." If you are trying to live on yesterday's revelation, it will not work for you. You have to be a man or woman of God and go where He leads you, regardless of who does or does not like it. You cannot make your decisions based on what everyone and their brother tells you to do.

I had to resign from some positions in a church I formerly attended because I had become filled with the Holy Spirit. My denomination didn't believe in it. In fact, they have made great waves around the world for not believing in it. They went to great lengths—publishing numerous manuscripts and books—telling the world why it was fundamentally impossible to have this experience. The only problem I had was the fact that I "experienced the experience" up close and personal! I know it to be true and available today. They were wrong then, and they are still wrong today. Our conversation may have gone something like this:

Them: "We don't accept you anymore."
Me: "That's all right. I'm going with God."
Them: "You do what you have to do."
Me: "I'm out of here. Call me history."
Them: "Well now, brother…"
Me: "Brother yourself! I'm gone."
Them: "Why?"
Me: "The old wineskins are crying too much."

Our Goal Is Loyalty

Faithfulness is only the starting point. God wants us to go beyond faithfulness. He wants us to reach higher to become loyal people. Let's go again to the relationship between Jonathan and David.

> So Jonathan made a covenant with the house of David, saying, Let the Lord even require it at the hand of David's enemies. And Jonathan caused David to swear again, because he loved him: for he loved him as he loved his own soul (1 Samuel 20:16-17).

This Scripture goes far beyond faithfulness. It's not easy to do, but that's what God wants from His people. If faithfulness is our goal, that's about as far as we will go, but I don't believe it should be our ultimate objective. It is only a required, entry-level form of Christianity.

A faithful man does what he says he will do, even in the face of inconvenience or hurt. Although every part of him may be screaming for a decision reversal, he carries on, cognizant that his word means too much to respond any other way. This is faithfulness regarding something you don't want to do. The Bible tells us that a faithful man "sweareth to his own hurt, and changeth not" (Psalm 15:4).

I am required to be faithful to everyone. I am required to be faithful to you whether I like you or not. I can be faithful to the entire body of Christ, but I cannot be

LOYALTY: GOING BEYOND FAITHFULNESS

loyal to every church, and certainly not to every person.

A person may tell you repeatedly that they are in covenant with you, and loyal to a fault. They may reiterate those words repeatedly over an extended span of time, but if their heart is not with you, they are doing nothing but blowing hot air in your face.

For example, would a pastor be considered faithful if they secretly sought a new position that offered more money or a better location? Still more, would they be faithful when they contacted various church committees or visited websites where churches post job openings? They could still be faithful to their congregation by standing in the pulpit each Sunday, but there would be a question of loyalty. Would they be loyal? They are physically there in the pulpit, but is their heart also there? I think not. That pastor's heart would possibly be trending to that big church in Honolulu with the five thousand members that contacted them last week for more information. Their heart-tie would be broken. As a result, they would still be faithful to their congregation by their presence alone, but that pastor would no longer be loyal to their church.

God requires a pastor to be loyal to his flock, but the congregation should not demand the pastor's loyalty if there isn't any loyalty shown to him by the congregation. I don't believe we can require anything from our leaders that we don't first require of ourselves.

Beyond Faithfulness Into Loyalty

I believe God wants us to go beyond faithfulness, however, and end up firmly established in the loyalty camp. Faithfulness is the minimum standard—the beginning. Let's look at some characteristics of each.

LOYALTY: GOING BEYOND FAITHFULNESS

CHAPTER 9

What Does Loyalty Look Like?

Church Member Loyalty

Every church has problems and challenges. Just as you and your family have problems, so does the church. The church has problems because people are involved, and people have problems. You need more money, a better car, and a bigger house. You need to buy school clothes for your children. Those are certainly problems and challenges we all face. That is just the way life is.

Do not complain about your church until you do something to address the issues that are causing you to complain. You may say, "But, our church has a lot of flaws in it." I hope that you are ready for a revelation:

so do you. Certainly every church has flaws in it, and I see them as well as you do. That is a characteristic of the body of Christ. There's no news there.

If you run away from your problems, you are disloyal. In fact, you are not even at the entry level of being faithful, much less becoming part of the answer.

Get a Job!

Faithfulness is a commendable quality that is difficult to find in people. A good church member needs a job or a task to do at church. You need it not simply because God wants you to be busy; you need it for your self-improvement, for discovering your gifts, and to lay up rewards in heaven. Don't come to church and just warm a seat; do something for the Lord.

If you are musically inclined, get involved in the music department. If your gift involves working with children or youth, serve God by working with them. It does not mean you take over those departments; it means you lend your support to them and be there to help those in leadership.

You should not expect to come into an established church and immediately oversee a department. Most of the time, there are people already in place and functioning in that capacity. It generally will take an undetermined amount of time to incorporate your gifts and talents into a ministry.

Make Your Leader Look Good

Faithfulness makes the organization look good. Loyalty makes the leader look good.

A person can actually believe in their organization and hate the leader. Loyalty makes the leadership look good. That's tough, isn't it? However, that's the truth.

Setting Your Promotion in Motion

You can go a long way to secure your first or next promotion if you will study this book and apply the knowledge and wisdom it contains into your daily thought life. The wonderful thing about the truths found in these pages is that they are all-encompassing; they are not merely relegated to the church. They will work in your chosen career path, and they will promote you in the workplace.

Have there been periods where you wondered why you can't seem to get ahead financially or even to secure a promotion at work? I'm sure you've wondered why other people have advanced beyond you. You may have found yourself mired in a slow-moving stream of mediocrity, and you don't like it! Realize that there is more to loyalty than merely showing up and punching the time clock. We have all seen people like that. Faithful as the clock itself, they punch in on time every day, stay and work hard all day long, but never get promoted. It's frustrating, but the good news is that there's a way out of your dissatisfaction.

LOYALTY: GOING BEYOND FAITHFULNESS

You must go beyond mere faithfulness. You need to know your boss—his or her likes, dislikes, and motivations—and strive to please them. Please note that I am certainly not referring to the use of shallow flattery to make an impression. Furthermore, you can't talk negatively about them behind their back and be loyal to them at the same time.

Killing Your Golden Goose

God did not call you into any organization to please your co-workers. He called you into that organization to please your employer. Be aware that there may be employees who will do nothing but grumble and complain about the organization, your boss, vacation time, or anything else they can come up with to cause discord. They want to entice you and draw you into their discontent. You could very easily become so disgruntled with that environment that you choose to leave that great "golden goose" of a job that God placed in your life. That job was God's answer to the prayers for your life. I've seen that happen many times over the years; so beware.

God is going to use a man—a human being—to be your "golden goose."

> Give, and it shall be given unto you; good measure, pressed down, and shaken together, and running over, shall **men** give into your bosom. For with the same measure that ye mete withal it shall be measured to you again (Luke 6:38, emphasis added).

What Does Loyalty Look Like?

God is not going to rain large bags of cash down on you from heaven while you sit on your front porch. God uses natural methods—a person, for example—as your source of supply from Him. So, go and be loyal!

LOYALTY: GOING BEYOND FAITHFULNESS

CHAPTER 10
What Does Loyalty Say?

Some people think that it's okay to listen to and participate in gossip all day long and still be considered a faithful person. Remember, faithfulness is only the beginning—the basic entry level. It is true that a faithful person should not listen to gossip, but taken one step further, a loyal person not only refuses to listen, but defends the victim who is being openly vilified.

You may say, "But I didn't enter into the conversation. I never said a word!" Maybe not, but did you step in and defend the one being denigrated? No? See, you may have been faithful, but you weren't loyal at all.

Put Out the Fire!

When an upset and disgruntled person comes to you with fire erupting from their ears, look at your hands. In one hand is a pitcher of water and in the other is a container full of gasoline. You then have a choice. You could pour gasoline on those red-hot words coming out of their mouth and make everything substantially worse, or you could do the right thing and let the water cool off the situation. It's your choice; be sure you make the right one.

Faithfulness comes to church and passively believes in a vision. Loyalty gets involved and actively helps to promote the vision. Faithfulness has many visions. Loyalty has one. Paul said, "This one thing I do" (Philippians 3:13).

One might say, "Well, I help everyone in the ministry." No, you are not helping as much as you could. If you don't have a place where you roll up your sleeves, become a part of the team, and actively participate in what's going on, you're not helping as you should.

The argument continues, "Well, I don't give just to the church I attend, I spread my tithe money around." While it is certainly a good thing that you're giving of your substance, you are not actually helping anyone as much as you could. You need to focus in on something and become part of it. Invest your time, effort, and money in it until it becomes a part of you. Hold on to it with tenacity, and let it permeate you. At that point, perhaps you will become loyal. However, until you reach that level, you're just hanging on, and punching the clock, spiritually speaking. You can give offerings wherever you choose, but your tithes should go to your local church—the place that feeds you.

I'm not trying to hurt you with these observations; I am only attempting to identify things for you. You must start with faithfulness, but you certainly should not end there.

A Loyal Pastor

"You are what you eat." I'm sure that you've heard that idiom many times. For example, if you constantly eat unhealthy food in large quantities, it can harm your health. Similarly, regularly eating healthy food in large quantities can also be detrimental to your health. You must come to the realization that your physical body needs a healthy and varied diet in normal quantities—a diet that has all the nutrients and building blocks of vitamins and minerals that you need.

Everyone knows that it's a good thing to get a balanced and varied diet. Scripture agrees that your spirit is a product of what you consume, and you need a varied diet there, too. Paul said it this way in the book of Acts, "For I have not shunned to declare unto you all the counsel of God" (Acts 20:27). He was saying that he made a habit of preaching on a variety of subjects.

The Role of the Pastor

If you are a traveling minister in a specialized area of ministry, you will normally only preach on certain topics. The role of the pastor is much different.

A loyal and responsible pastor can't preach on only one subject exclusively. The role of the pastor is to lead the sheep beside still waters and into green pastures. David writes, "He maketh me to lie down in green pastures: he leadeth me beside the still waters" (Psalm 23:2). He must provide his flock with a proper diet, full of the many nutrients required for proper growth.

A loyal pastor feeds and helps nourish the flock of God correctly. They must water and tend to the flock so that they become strong and spiritually healthy.

Some subjects or concepts that the pastor teaches should only be a small part of the flock's overall diet. A loyal pastor doesn't teach the same subject over and over; he rotates through different subjects. A pastor should teach one subject and then set it aside and teach something else entirely. As a caveat, subjects are often combined, and it works quite well. For example, the local flock needs a steady diet of faith. It's very easy, and necessary, to mix the subject of faith in with the topics of healing or prosperity; they are related. In fact, faith can be sprinkled in with everything taught, but the subject of faith doesn't need to be taught exclusively all the time.

A loyal pastor also needs to teach about money from time to time, because that's where the devil snares many of us. The subject of finances needs to be covered at least once a year, but probably more.

The subject of relationships—how to effectively relate to people—needs to be covered regularly. In addition, teachings on home-life and family are needed so the church can keep their lives in order.

Each time these subjects are taught they don't need to be a rerun. In many cases, the second, third, and subsequent sermons are designed to water the seed that was planted by the first lesson. One person sows the Word; another person waters it, and God gives the increase.

> I have planted, Apollos watered; but God gave the increase. So then neither is he that planteth any thing, neither he that watereth; but God that giveth the increase (1 Corinthians 3:6-7).

LOYALTY: GOING BEYOND FAITHFULNESS

CHAPTER 11
Loyalty Goes the Extra Mile

Faithfulness can be counted on. People say, "I was there. I was on time." That's fine, faithful Christian. However, loyalty is trustworthy to do what is needed.

Faithfulness does a task. They say, "I teach children in Sunday School." That's good, faithful Christian. Loyalty performs a service; it cares for people. Think of that loyal Sunday School teacher, all alone, down on her knees, praying, "God, give me a word for these little children. God, I pray for little Sally. I know her home life is in chaos. God, today let me be an encouragement in her life. Let me say something from You that would help her."

LOYALTY: GOING BEYOND FAITHFULNESS

Although being faithful is good, we have known all too many task-oriented people like the faithful teacher. What we need is an influx of servants of the Lord, like the loyal teacher.

Loyalty's Freedom

Faithfulness understands submission. Many people don't, but faithful people do. Loyalty, however, understands love and the place it holds in loyal relationships. It goes beyond submission. Loyalty says, "God, I love my pastor, and I believe he loves me. Maybe I don't understand everything he does, but I believe in his integrity."

Faithfulness does not speak against leadership. Loyalty not only refuses to speak against leadership, but it also speaks favorably concerning them. It's one thing not to speak evil, but it's another thing altogether to speak favorably.

Faithfulness is required, but loyalty is expected. Loyalty is the tie of the heart. When loyalty is broken, the heart-tie is broken.

We must go beyond being faithful people and become loyal people. We must be loyal to a cause. We must be loyal to a vision. We must be loyal to our leadership.

This faithfulness versus loyalty conversation may sound like bondage to you, but as the Bible says in the fourth chapter of Mark, "If any man have ears to hear, let him hear" (Mark 4:23). Loyalty can mean freedom for you.

God Became Involved

As we have seen, one of the greatest examples of a relationship that went beyond faithfulness was the relationship between David and Jonathan. Their relationship was holy. God Himself became involved in their lives. It was a holy relationship between two masculine, brave, and courageous men—neither one weak or effeminate. We read in 1 Samuel:

> And it came to pass, when he had made an end of speaking unto Saul, that the soul of Jonathan was knit with the soul of David, and Jonathan loved him as his own soul (1 Samuel 18:1).

David and Jonathan had a heart-tie or soul-tie. You've heard the phrase "soul mates." They were soul mates. They had come into a relationship with one another that allowed them to be close, to share trusted information, and to become comrades in the faith. It was a great relationship—a truly holy thing.

We saw in First Samuel, chapter eighteen, that David didn't return home to his father but stayed in the palace at Jonathan's request. David and Jonathan subsequently made a covenant together.

> And Saul took him that day, and would let him go no more home to his father's house. Then Jonathan and David made a covenant, because he loved him as his own soul (1 Samuel 18:2-3).

Tests of Loyalty

Some years ago, a man who worked for me said, "I believe the Lord wants us to be like David and Jonathan." Let me say that I'm open to the Lord, but I'm certainly not gullible. So, I said, "All right, if that's what God wants, we'll let Him bring it to pass."

The Lord is not going to force you into that kind of relationship. Just because someone else wants it, it's not going to be imposed on you. A faithful person, as we discussed, is faithful across the board, but loyalty is something beyond that, and it is not given to everyone.

Sometimes, you may find your loyalty to a person tested. If you are married, your spouse is the most important relationship that you have. If a person speaks against my wife, Nora, my loyalty to her demands that I defend her. I can't be loyal to the other person over my wife. Above anyone else on this planet, my loyalty is to her. I will not allow people to speak against her. You might think I'm touchy, but that is how loyalty responds. You should be that way, too.

Passionate Defense

You need to be a passionate and courageous person, possessing enough gumption and courage to allow some things—very important, significant things—to upset you. When Jesus turned over the moneychanger's tables in the temple and ran them out with a whip, do you think He was happy with them? Not that day! He was more than righteously indignant.

Loyalty Goes the Extra Mile

Jesus was upset because He had a passion for the kingdom of God and His Father's work. His loyalty was to the Father before it was to any other person. He loved His mother, His disciples, and everyone else, and He was faithful to all of them; however, His loyalty above everything else was to God, His Father. If you found yourself trying to obstruct that loyalty, you'd get on the wrong side of Jesus in a hurry.

Peter was the first person in the Bible who gave us a great revelation of the Lord with this insight: "And Simon Peter answered and said, Thou art the Christ, the Son of the living God" (Matthew 16:16). Because of Peter's insight into that revelation, Jesus blessed him.

> And Jesus answered and said unto him, Blessed art thou, Simon Barjona: for flesh and blood hath not revealed it unto thee, but my Father which is in heaven (Matthew 16:17).

Then, a few verses later, as Jesus was preparing for a trip to Jerusalem, Peter admonished Him over concerns for His safety. In response, Jesus rebuked Peter:

> From that time forth began Jesus to shew unto his disciples, how that he must go unto Jerusalem, and suffer many things of the elders and chief priests and scribes, and be killed, and be raised again the third day. Then Peter took him, and began to rebuke

him, saying, Be it far from thee, Lord: this shall not be unto thee. But he turned, and said unto Peter, Get thee behind me, Satan: thou art an offence unto me: for thou savourest not the things that be of God, but those that be of men (Matthew 16:21-23).

It was Jesus' passion and loyalty to His Father and His Father's work—above all else—that determined the things that angered Him.

Discern Before Listening

Choose who you are going to let speak into your life. There are only certain people who I have given the right to speak into mine. I also do not believe that just anyone has the right to correct you. Don't be a garbage dump for everyone.

Through faithfulness and loyalty, you can decide who has the right to speak into your life at certain levels. I don't think everyone has that privilege, so don't open yourself up to just anyone. Allowing everyone access will not necessarily keep you from error. In all actuality, too many voices could lead you into error much faster because of the diversity of advice given.

I only allow people I know and trust to speak into my life, not just anyone off the street. Moreover, if I truly believe they care about me, I must be willing to listen to my trusted advisers even when they tell me something that I don't necessarily want to hear.

Loyalty Goes the Extra Mile

Scripture says, "Faithful are the wounds of a friend; but the kisses of an enemy are deceitful" (Proverbs 27:6).

Think about Judas. One moment he was eating with Jesus and the next he was handing Him over to those who wanted to kill Him. One moment he was kissing the Lord and the next he was sacrificing Him. Some people have the propensity to be friendly to you and harbor selfish motives that hurt you at the same time!

It is important to realize that the depth by which you hear from God will be commensurate with the degree that devils will talk to you. The more you hear from God, the more discernment you need to recognize the voice of an evil spirit.

Remember the employee who told me he believed our relationship was going to be like David and Jonathan's? In only a matter of weeks, one of the worst betrayals I've ever known came through that man. He used holy things to get on the inside track. That supposed relationship was phony, pretentious, and contrived; but, David and Jonathan's was genuine.

LOYALTY: GOING BEYOND FAITHFULNESS

CHAPTER 12
A Holy Covenant

> And Jonathan stripped himself of the robe that was upon him, and gave it to David, and his garments even to his sword, and to his bow, and to his girdle (1 Samuel 18:4).

When people entered into a covenant in Bible times, they would exchange gifts as a token or sign of that covenant. That's exactly what was happening in this verse. We see that Jonathan removed his outer apparel, sword, and bow and gave them to David. They were exchanging seals of this particular covenant relationship.

Covenants are still entered into daily. For instance, your wedding ring represents a gift to your wife or husband that signifies the covenant of marriage that you entered. Malachi says that the Lord, Himself, was witness to the covenant made with your marriage vows.

> Yet you ask, Why does He reject it? Because the Lord was witness [to the covenant made at your marriage] between you and the wife of your youth, against whom you have dealt treacherously and to whom you were faithless. Yet she is your companion and the wife of your covenant [made by your marriage vows] (Malachi 2:14, AMP).

The wedding ring doesn't have to be expensive for the covenant of marriage to be enacted. In fact, it could be a very inexpensive token of your love for your wife or husband. It is not the cost of the ring that matters; the important thing is what it represents and what it says. It signifies that there is a person with whom I am in covenant.

Besides being considered the closest finger to your heart, according to ancient folklore, there was a belief that a vein from the fourth finger of the left hand ran directly to the heart. The vein came to be known as the "*vena amoris*" that translates as "the vein of love." As a result, the fourth finger of the left hand has been labeled "the love finger." Forever tied to the heart, that's where the engagement and wedding rings reside. When you put a ring on that finger, it is an indication of a covenant—a heart-tie—with someone. It's a great visual representation of two hearts being connected by covenant.

There are different types of covenants, but they all usually exchange gifts. David and Jonathan were in a different type of covenant relationship. It wasn't a marriage, but it was a covenant relationship just the same.

Jonathan's Magnanimous Gesture

In Jonathan's case of being heir-apparent to the throne, the act of giving the robe and the armor to David meant that he was submitting himself to the recognition that David, not he, had been given the throne by God. That was a serious and sober thing. He was saying, "I recognize on whom the anointing of the Lord rests, and I am willing to go along with God's choice." He was submitting this holy relationship to the will of God. The hearts of these men were firmly knit together by the Spirit of the Lord, and so they made a covenant.

Remember, Saul lost the anointing of God to be king, and David received it. Saul recognized it, and he was angry enough to want David dead. He set out to kill him, but Jonathan's loyalty led him to warn David of Saul's plan.

When Disobedience is Proper

The Bible says children should obey their parents. However, we cannot honor our parents beyond the will of God. The Bible also tells us to honor our leaders; similarly, we do not honor our leaders above the known and revealed will of God.

No matter who the leaders are, if they violate the Word of God, they are just as guilty as anyone else would be who violated it. We honor their office, but we do not have to honor their ungodly behavior. That is an important distinction. It does not mean we do violence or harm, but it does mean that the law of God is higher than any other law.

Jonathan tried to reason with his father because he could see that Saul was making a terrible mistake. He knew that Saul was wrong, and he refused to take his father's side. Instead, he reminded Saul of David's goodness, and he warned the king that it would be a sin to harm David.

Loyal to the Covenant

Here you see Jonathan, who through loyalty to his covenant, defended his covenant brother, David, against evil. When you are loyal to someone, you defend that person in the face of their enemies.

> And I will go out and stand beside my father in the field where thou art, and I will commune with my father of thee; and what I see, that I will tell thee. And Jonathan spake good of David unto Saul his father, and said unto him, Let not the king sin against his servant, against David;

because he hath not sinned against thee, and because his works have been to thee-ward very good: (1 Samuel 19:3-4).

Saul was David's chief enemy, but David's loyalty to his king caused David to continue to speak well of him. If you take sides with someone who is speaking evil of a person that you are supposed to be loyal to—and you don't speak up—you're not loyal! You must defend that person. You must defend them even if you lose friendships over your decision. Sometimes it isn't easy to be loyal. Let's look at the fourth verse again.

> And Jonathan spake good of David unto Saul his father, and said unto him, Let not the king sin against his servant, against David; because he hath not sinned against thee, and because his works have been to thee-ward very good: (1 Samuel 19:4).

Jonathan defended David. He reminded his father, King Saul, what a tremendous asset David had proven to be to him over time. What Jonathan was trying to say was, "Dad, you're getting ready to kill the goose that lays your golden eggs!"

Speaking Against Leadership

When you talk against leadership, you might be killing that same golden "goose" that is feeding your spiritual life. When your soul-tie is broken, the spiritual umbilical cord goes with it.

When you hear statements like this, "Well, I don't receive anything at church. I believe the pastor has lost his anointing." If you'll be honest—gut-level honest—it's probably not the pastor who has lost the anointing. Instead, you have probably lost your anointed ear to hear what he is saying!

The soul-tie, or the tie of the heart, is what brings the flow of the anointing. When we become disloyal or become a party to disloyalty, that "feeding line" or spiritual umbilical cord is broken. That's when you can't receive. You can hear the Word and memorize the sermons, but that's not enough.

Look at what the Bible says in the book of Mark, "If any man have ears to hear, let him hear" (Mark 4:23). The whole congregation hears the words of the sermon, but only the person who has an ear to hear can hear and understand the true meaning of the message.

Jonathan's Loyalty

In this passage, Jonathan continues speaking to Saul, his father:

> For he did put his life in his hand, and slew the Philistine, and the Lord wrought a great salvation for all Israel: thou sawest it, and didst rejoice: wherefore then wilt thou sin against innocent blood, to slay David without a cause? And Saul hearkened unto the voice of Jonathan: and

> Saul sware, As the Lord liveth, he shall not be slain. And Jonathan called David, and Jonathan shewed him all those things. And Jonathan brought David to Saul, and he was in his presence, as in times past (1 Samuel 19:5-7).

Unfortunately, Saul's change of heart did not last. His rage, once again, eventually overtook him. David had to run for his life and hide from Saul. Through it all, however, Jonathan stayed true to David.

Signs of a Covenant Relationship

This passage demonstrates how a covenant relationship—a loyal relationship—operates: "Then said Jonathan unto David, Whatsoever thy soul desireth, I will even do it for thee" (1 Samuel 20:4). In the everyday, everyman, Ed King translation, Jonathan was saying, "Whatever you want me to do, David, I'll do it. I've got your back."

I have a few friends like that. If I called them in the middle of the night, they would drop whatever they were doing—probably sleeping, just like I would be if the roles were reversed—and do anything for me. Some of them live hundreds of miles away, but they wouldn't hesitate to do whatever I asked them to do. They would do it based solely on the fact that I asked and nothing more.

If you travel with friends as I do, one of two things will happen to your relationship. You become either

LOYALTY: GOING BEYOND FAITHFULNESS

very close or quite distant. I have traveled the world with companions that over time have grown to know me well as I have grown to know them. We have become extremely compatible.

We can certainly be faithful to everyone, but we cannot have a relationship based on loyalty with everyone. It's not based on luck, chemistry, or the ability to get along; it's more than that. It's a soul-tie —a spiritual tie. It's a relationship that the Lord gives us and is certainly not one we will share with every friend we have. Everyone should have that type of relationship in the spirit with your leadership and your pastor.

"Does that mean if I call my pastor at any time of the day or night, he should drop everything and show up?" No. What it means is you should never call your pastor unless you have a very real need. Then, as the pastor, whatever you're asked to do, you should trust your friend enough to believe it's absolutely necessary.

However, if we are disloyal in our hearts, we can never have that kind of relationship. The trust factor is gone. The soul-tie is gone. The heart connection is gone. You become only a church attendee and not a covenant participant.

CHAPTER 13

Protecting Loyalties

You must protect your relationships. I may love you, but if you speak against my wife, Nora, we are going to have trouble. Is that sin? No, because my priority is to her. For the same reason, if you speak against the Lord, we are also going to have trouble.

I was in a business establishment recently, and a guy had an accident. As a result, he started cursing incessantly, "God blank this and God blank that," as well as a few other choice profanities. I thought the paint was going to peel off the wall! After the third or fourth salvo of verbal assaults, I looked around and saw that he was talking to me. He was talking to the wrong guy, now.

I said, "Why are you cursing the Lord, man? He didn't do this to you. You did it to yourself." He said, "Oh yeah?" I said, in a tone that could never be interpreted as timid, "That's exactly right." He shut up and looked like a whipped pup. He never said one more word, and I never said one more word to him, either. The conversation was over. Why? My loyalty was not to him; my loyalty was to the Lord. This man was speaking against someone I love—someone who has my allegiance.

There ought to be people in your life with whom you share that same kind of loyalty. Of course, your first loyalty is to God. However, the next person you should be loyal to is your spouse. As I stated before, I do not allow people to speak against my wife. It's just not going to happen.

Ranking Loyalties

You cannot bring a friend into your life that has priority over your husband or wife. You can have a covenant partner like we have been describing, but you cannot put that friend above a higher covenant.

You cannot put that friend above God. If you do, God will take them out of your life, and you will lose that relationship. Neither can you put that friendship above your covenant partner—your spouse—or God will take that person out of your life for violating spiritual principles.

In the economy of God, if you have a spiritual leader—and you are supposed to have one—there is no one on the planet who has the right to speak to you against that person. If they do and you don't do something about it, you will lose that heart-tie.

You may be faithful, but are you loyal?

If you believe the Spirit of God has sent someone into your life to speak the oracles of God and instruct you in the ways of the Lord, you are unwise to let anyone speak against them. Protect that relationship at all costs.

Even if the person being attacked does not hold a covenant relationship with you, if God has chosen them to speak into your life, you still must be faithful to them. You must be faithful to everyone; that is entry-level Christianity. However, if that person holds that esteemed position of giving spiritual input to you, dear brother and sister, that is a holy thing, and you must protect it. If the heart-tie exists, they would be wrong to be disloyal to you as well.

Your Next Step in the Lord

Loyalty is your next step in the Lord. Do you ever go beyond entry-level faithfulness into loyalty? When you have a guest speaker in your church or organization, do you come and support the meeting? You may not know them, and you may not like them, but you must be loyal to your group.

The late Dr. Lester Sumrall, considered one of the great faith leaders of the twentieth century, was a great mentor to me. In fact, He ordained me. He preached and spoke at our church many times over the years, and I found him engaging in every way. He took a great interest in me as a young preacher just starting out in the ministry, and I will never forget it. Although he is in heaven today, my loyalty remains with him.

The last time Dr. Sumrall was at our church, another traveling minister who had never met Dr. Sumrall joined us at my home for a late meal. This minister shared about his ministry. He said, "Dr. Sumrall, I have a ministry to a certain group that ministers to some very prominent people." Not impressed in the slightest, Dr. Sumrall looked at him and responded in his particular fashion, "Humph. I'd rather feed hungry babies." The room fell so silent that you could hear the trees grow. Dr. Sumrall was intensely loyal to God and the gospel, not just to prominent people.

Totally Focused

To say that Dr. Lester Sumrall was totally focused would be an understatement. As far as he was concerned, if you did anything different from what he did, you were wasting time. To him, what he did was the most important thing. That's the way you ought to live your life as well. You ought to think that what you're doing is "it."

When you establish true loyalties in your life, many of the hardest decisions you will ever make will have already been decided for you. No one has the right to speak into my life against my established lines of loyalty. If they do, they are not of God. A person could certainly say that they were sent from the Lord, but if they speak against those to whom I'm loyal, I automatically know that there's a problem. They couldn't be sent from the Lord because God established those lines, and He wouldn't violate them.

Restoration

When pressure comes once your lines of loyalty are established, you have no choice but to walk in them.

If sin was to enter your life, your path of restoration is already established, based on your loyalties. For example, if you were involved in an adulterous relationship, and that relationship was made public, your restoration would be through your established lines of loyalty. You couldn't go to another town and hide.

You may hear, "I understand, but I want to run and hide. I want to be ten thousand miles away from here." I understand. Everyone wants to run and hide. But if you want to be what you are supposed to be in God and regain your place in Him that you lost because of sin, there are not two places to do it. The place where you committed the sin is the one and only place of restoration.

No one wants to do it this way. That's why you must establish lines of restoration before you get under that pressure so they become the guide of what to do. It doesn't mean you have to stay in that place forever, but it does mean restoration entails a process. You can't complete the process if you don't face the issue where it happened.

Dealing with Sin

I am in a visible public ministry. If I fell into adultery, my restoration would need to be public—all but the private details, obviously. I would have an obligation and responsibility to repent to the people that I defrauded. If there is any chance for me to become what I am supposed to be in God, repentance has to be genuine.

You have to face the proverbial music. Sending someone to another city for an unspecified length of time and then declaring them restored upon their return is doing nothing more than covering up the sin and pretending it never happened.

You can't be a man or a woman of God unless you make the hard calls in the crisis hour.

Ministerial Loyalty

If you have been ordained through and have received papers from, a particular ministry, you must be loyal to that ministry. There are times, however, when changes happen that need addressing in a proper way.

Many years ago, my original ordination was through a denomination whose beliefs I agreed with at the time but came to a point where I didn't agree with them totally. I received the baptism of the Holy Spirit while I was heavily involved in that particular denomination—the same denomination that did not recognize the baptism of the Holy Spirit in their core beliefs. Now, what was I supposed to do? It happened! I'm filled—denomination or not. I had no other choice; in order to be in agreement, I had to remove myself and realign with an organization that I could agree with. I wanted to be ordained by a body of believers that I could be loyal to, so I was re-ordained.

Loyalty to Your Church

Faithfulness is great, but God demands something beyond it. Loyalty is a hot button. It's a hot issue with God. If you are part of a church, you ought to be loyal to the things that go on in that church.

For example, if you are experiencing an internal conflict about whether or not to go to a concert on a date that conflicts with a church service, it's because you haven't established your loyalty lines. Establish loyalty lines and conflicts disappear.

You may firmly believe that you really need to attend that concert. I'm not saying you shouldn't go, but if you have responsibilities at church that you are expected to perform, those obligations need to be given serious consideration.

Loyalty in Finances

Faithfulness gives tithes. Loyalty gives tithes plus offerings. There's a big difference between giving tithes and giving offerings. You tithe because the Bible instructs you to, and you want the blessing attached to it. But, an offering goes deeper. You give an offering because you believe in a cause, and you believe in what the church or ministry is doing; you simply want to help.

When your church receives an offering for something—chairs, equipment, paving the parking lot or building a sanctuary—loyalty responds with a financial donation. Loyalty may even respond with multiple gifts. The faithful Christian, on the other hand, may be content just to give tithes.

The Body of Christ has million-dollar needs and ten-dollar commitments. The math doesn't work, and that's a problem. Many people want to come and receive from the Lord, but they don't have any desire to be loyal and give of their substance to the church. They don't put their faith in it, believe in it, pray for it, and they certainly don't want to sweat for it.

There are half a dozen ministries I support personally in addition to my church, but the bulk of my giving is to the church I pastor. Why? This is where my loyalties are. I put the bulk of my giving in the church because I believe in what goes on here, not just because I'm the pastor. Jesus said, "For where your treasure is, there will your heart be also" (Matthew 6:21). I put it here because that is where my heart is.

If you are a member or even attend a church and you do not give to that church, you are not loyal there. As a result, you cut off the revelation of God that you should be experiencing. Please don't take that wrong, but it is the truth. If you see enough things happen over the years, you learn things, even if you don't have a Bible verse for them. Truth, as the saying goes, is where you find it. The Bible says that wisdom cries in the streets.

I have found over the process of years that the majority of people who cause problems in the church have at least one thing in common; they are not contributing anything, financially or otherwise, to the church. They gripe and complain about any number of things—the direction of the church, the color of the carpet, the pastor's clothes, the pastor's car—it doesn't matter what it is. They didn't contribute anything, so I have to ask: what do they have to complain about?

People who do not give anything to their church are not loyal to it. Their loyalties are divided. They are confused in their minds and hearts. They are double-minded which impacts their priorities, and they tend to find fault.

They don't understand that there is a vision. They don't understand that there is a reason for decisions that are made. They don't understand that someone in leadership has given the issue a great amount of thought and prayer and has come up with a plan—a strategy of implementation. Loyalty causes many internal conflicts to cease because priorities have already been established.

Loyalty to Leadership

From where I stand, I won't allow people to speak against my leaders in the faith or the faith message. I know there are possibly some errors that happened in the past with immature people hearing incorrectly. I know there can be some extremes, but all movements have these problems. All of them can get a little twisted and a little bent over time.

I am not referring to being gullible and falling for just anything. Even if I did see an extreme in a situation, I might pray about it or talk to the person involved, but I would not talk about it publicly.

At one point, when I was floundering for the direction that I sorely needed as a young preacher, the faith message became the stream of God's blessing in my life. It totally changed my direction and my life. It changed everything about me. For me to leave now and get into something else would be impossible. Where would I go? There is no other place to go.

So I am loyal to the faith message, even though I understand that not everything in it is perfect or ideal. Nevertheless, I am loyal to it. Your loyalties will determine where you stand on issues. Your loyalties will determine what makes you righteously indignant. This principle of loyalty is the thin line that will change your life. Don't speak against it.

Loyalty Is a Servant

This conversation is recorded in Scripture, "Then said Jonathan unto David, Whatsoever thy soul desireth, I will even do it for thee" (1 Samuel 20:4). Loyalty becomes a servant. A loyal person says, "I'll do what you ask me to do because you asked me to do it, and I don't have to have another reason." You don't even have to apologize. Understand, however, that for loyalty to be that absolute, the person who is on the receiving end cannot ask unless there is a genuine need.

> And as soon as the lad was gone, David arose out of a place toward the south, and fell on his face to the ground, and bowed himself three times: and they kissed one another, and wept one with another, until David exceeded. And Jonathan said to David, Go in peace, forasmuch as we have sworn both of us in the name of the Lord, saying, The Lord be between me and thee, and between my seed and thy seed for ever. And he arose and departed: and Jonathan went into the city (1 Samuel 20:41-42).

Notice that they basically said, "This covenant we are in is not only with us, but it is with our families. We are in a family covenant."

LOYALTY: GOING BEYOND FAITHFULNESS

You know the story: Jonathan lost his life not too long after this, and David eventually became king. Even though Jonathan was dead, David's loyalty to him and his family continued. Again we see that to honor the covenant, David sought out Jonathan's son, Mephibosheth, to show him favor.

> Now when Mephibosheth, the son of Jonathan, the son of Saul, was come unto David, he fell on his face, and did reverence. And David said, Mephibosheth. And he answered, Behold thy servant! And David said unto him, Fear not: for I will surely shew thee kindness for Jonathan thy father's sake, and will restore thee all the land of Saul thy father; and thou shalt eat bread at my table continually. And he bowed himself, and said, What is thy servant, that thou shouldest look upon such a dead dog as I am? Then the king called to Ziba, Saul's servant, and said unto him, I have given unto thy master's son all that pertained to Saul and to all his house. Thou therefore, and thy sons, and thy servants, shall till the land for him, and thou shalt bring in the fruits, that thy master's son may have food to eat: but Mephibosheth thy master's son shall eat bread alway at my table. Now Ziba had fifteen sons and twenty servants. Then said Ziba unto the king, According to all that my lord the king hath commanded his servant, so shall thy servant do. As for Mephibosheth, said the

king, he shall eat at my table, as one of the king's sons. And Mephibosheth had a young son, whose name was Micha. And all that dwelt in the house of Ziba were servants unto Mephibosheth. So Mephibosheth dwelt in Jerusalem: for he did eat continually at the king's table; and was lame on both his feet (2 Samuel 9:6-13).

Jonathan's son was crippled, and David took him in. It wouldn't have mattered if Mephibosheth had been a beggar; David honored Jonathan by observing the covenant they had made, even after Jonathan's death. That's the kind of loyalty God wants in His people. You cannot make this type of commitment with just anyone unless the Lord gives it to you.

You need to make this type of commitment first to God, then to your spouse, and then to your spiritual leader. Outside of that, you can make such a commitment only as God gives the relationship.

David was the king; he didn't have to do all that for Jonathan's son. Who was going to make him do it? Jonathan wasn't there to remind him, either. However, David had integrity, and he remembered their covenant. He knew what he and Jonathan had together. It was David's heart that made him respond that way.

LOYALTY: GOING BEYOND FAITHFULNESS

CHAPTER 14
Faithfulness vs. Loyalty

- Faithfulness is a characteristic, or character trait, which is learned. Loyalty goes much deeper and emanates from the heart.

- Faithfulness can be a mechanical response. Loyalty has integrity as its base. Proverbs 11:3 says, "The integrity of the upright shall guide them."

- Faithfulness does what is required. Loyalty does what is right.

For example, a loyal person, seeing an incidental amount of litter in the parking lot, will go out of their way to pick it up. A faithful person would possibly need instruction to do that. Loyalty does not need instruction; it sees the issue and takes care of it on its own.

- Faithfulness starts on time and leaves on time because it is a requirement of good stewardship. Loyalty, recognizing the possibility of a potential need, comes early in case someone needs help. Loyalty comes early and stays late.

- Faithfulness finishes the task. Loyalty goes the extra mile. Loyalty polishes it, puts a bow on it, and leaves it better than it was.

- Faithfulness does what it can. Loyalty does what it takes to get the job done.

- Faithfulness does what is expected. Loyalty exceeds expectations and does the unexpected.

- Faithfulness does its job and does it well. Loyalty does more than its job. It finds options that create extra value.

- Faithfulness doesn't exploit or point out weaknesses. Loyalty, on the other hand, covers weaknesses and helps strengthen them.

- Faithfulness recognizes needs. Loyalty offers solutions.

- Faithfulness believes in pastors. Loyalty has only one; it doesn't share between two or more.

Faithfulness vs. Loyalty

- Faithfulness gives the entry-level tithe. Loyalty demands more commitment.

- Faithfulness moves when the crowd moves. Loyalty moves when the leader moves. Some may say, "Well, I'm a participant in the church. I go along with the crowd." Maybe God wants you to do more than just "go along." Maybe He wants you to bring someone else along!

- Faithfulness needs motivation. Loyalty motivates. Loyalty says, "Let's go! We can do it!"

- Faithfulness only does what it says it will do. Loyalty amends the contract and does what it takes, over and above what's expected, at no charge.

- Faithfulness has a vision. Loyalty promotes it.

- Faithfulness will call you on the phone. Loyalty will call you, then come to your house and pray with you.

- Faithfulness will keep records. Loyalty will cry with you.

- Faithfulness will count the numbers. Loyalty will count the tears.

- Faithfulness believes in being blessed, but loyalty believes in being a blessing.

LOYALTY: GOING BEYOND FAITHFULNESS

You are blessed to be a blessing. This verse in Genesis shows God's willingness to bless those who bless.

> Now the Lord had said unto Abram, Get thee out of thy country, and from thy kindred, and from thy father's house, unto a land that I will shew thee: And I will make of thee a great nation, and I will bless thee, and make thy name great; and thou shalt be a blessing: And I will bless them that bless thee, and curse him that curseth thee: and in thee shall all families of the earth be blessed (Genesis 12:1-3).

Final Challenge

Faithfulness is great, but God wants more. He wants to pull more out of us. Faithfulness is entry-level Christianity—entry-level service to God. The Lord wants us to go beyond faithfulness and become loyal people, having a sense of community, a sense of belonging, a sense of purpose, and a sense of destiny.

About the Author

DR. ED KING is the founder and Senior Pastor of Redemption Church in Knoxville, Tennessee. In addition to pastoring, Dr. King is president of *The Power of the Word* television ministry, which is broadcast both nationally and internationally to a potential audience of over one billion people. He resides in Knoxville along with his wife and co-pastor, Nora. Their daughter Laren and son-in-law Adam also work with them in full-time ministry.

In addition to pastoring Redemption Church and his lead role at *Power of the Word*, Pastor King travels extensively, and he has ministered in over sixty nations around the world, teaching, and preaching the gospel to thousands of people in leadership conferences and evangelistic meetings. Pastor King is the author of several books which include: ***Will My Pet Be in Heaven?***, ***Loyalty: Going Beyond Faithfulness***, and ***God's Timing: His Timetable for Your Life***.

Available at Redemption Church, your local bookstore or online.

WILL MY PET BE IN HEAVEN?
by Dr. Ed King

We adore our pets, and they become family; so, when they pass on, we suffer great loss. Dr. Ed King gives us solid, biblical answers to this often asked question. He shows us from the Bible about the past, current, and future existence of animals in heaven, as well as their ultimate purpose. Finally, an exhaustive answer for a question that always comes up!

ISBN: 9781602730687 • 93 pages • $8.95.

LOYALTY
Going Beyond Faithfulness
by Dr. Ed King

CHRISTIANITY 101 calls us to imitate our Father God, but maturity calls us into loyalty. In this book, Pastor King elaborates on the subtle distinctions between faithfulness and loyalty and focuses on lessons learned by looking at the brotherly love shared by Jonathan and David. Find promotion and honor as you commit to be a rare gem in God's crown who demonstrates both of these desirable traits. It all starts with a decision!
ISBN: 9781602730793 • 110 pages • $8.95.

3550 Pleasant Ridge Road

Knoxville, TN 37921

865.521.7777

www.redemptionchurch.com

RedemptionChurchTN   RedemptionChurchTN   RedemptionTN

PO Box 52466

Knoxville, TN 37950

1.800.956.4433

www.poweroftheword.com

powbroadcast   powbroadcast

10 Major Life Lessons—CD series
This series will upgrade your life in every way. You'll learn the power of a seed, the importance of forgiveness, how to live a disciplined life, and much more. Apply these valuable ten lessons to your own life, and you'll go further than you ever thought possible.

Conquering Life's Limitations—CD series
As Christians, we have the mind of Christ and there are no limitations on what God can reveal and show to you if we're open to it. Listen as Pastor Nora King explains how wisdom is the most important thing to us if we want to conquer life's limitations.

Divine Healing and the Atonement—CD series
Do you need healing in your life? Are you aware of the healing power that is available to you? In Pastor King's message, you can discover: the true meaning of Jesus' atonement, and how Jesus satisfied the judgement against us to bring us righteousness and healing

Faith: How May It Help You?—CD series
God never intended for His family to live a life of lack, struggle or constant defeat. He sent His Word to rescue us and He gave FAITH as a tool to overcome the obstacles we face. We can take the gift of faith, and by activating it and using it, we can create an exciting and victorious life.

Grace vs. Works—CD series
For by grace we are saved through faith—it is a gift of God, not of works. Grace verses works—they both have to be looked at; they have to be thought about; and they have to be considered. Both are biblical truths and are important to believers.

Heaven—CD series
We hear a lot about Heaven. What does the Bible say about it? This 11-part series establishes a foundational truth on our future home. Heaven is a real place; a place to look forward to. Insightful teachings like these are a must for every believer.

How to Study the Bible—CD series
Every Christian knows it's good to read the Bible; but, how often do we understand the depths of what we're reading? In this series, you'll learn some of the personal study habits and recommended study tools of a man with 30 years of experience in learning the Bible and a ministry for teaching.

Keeping Hope Alive—CD series
In this series, the importance of keeping hope alive is revealed, along with many ways we misplace our hope and how to break through the bondage of despair. You will also discover that hope is a vital part of who you are in Christ.

Truth: Your Baseline for Life—CD series
Listen to this 5-CD series by Pastor Ed King and discover how truth relates to your freedom, relationships, growth in character, wisdom, and much more. You can begin today to live a life of power and liberty.

Walking in Divine Favor—CD series
In this CD series, Pastor Ed King teaches keys to living in favor with God and man. Learn the importance of honor and integrity in relationships, cheerful giving, grateful receiving, and more. The keys listed in this insightful series will move you forward faster than you can move yourself alone.

Parsons Publishing House
Your Voice Your World™

30 DAYS TO A BETTER PRAYER LIFE
by Pastor Nora King
Nora King offers fresh revelation and practical teaching to help you experience the release of God's power. You will learn daily how to improve your prayer life and enter God's presence through these simple principles. You don't have to struggle in prayer any longer!
ISBN: 9781602730120 • 142 pages • $11.95.

JESUS IN 3D
by Pastor Robert Gay
Do you want to expose the life of God in every aspect of your life? If you want to reflect the life of God, you must receive and activate all that He did, everything He said, and everything He demonstrated. Pastor Robert Gay uncovers how God's grace actually empowers your prayers to be answered, your joy to be unleashed, and your life to be blessed as you shine as a reflection of Jesus in the earth.
ISBN: 9781602730588 • 104 pages • $9.95.

Parsons Publishing House
Your Voice Your World™

Available at your local bookstore or order online at www.Amazon.com

Parsons Publishing House
Your Voice Your World ™

AVAILABLE IN BOOKSTORES AND ONLINE

70 REASONS FOR SPEAKING IN TONGUES
Your Own Built in Spiritual Dynamo
by Dr. BiLL Hamon
ISBN: 9781602730137 • 216 pages • $14.95 USD.

UpRIGHTing RELATIONSHIPS
by Linda Roeder
ISBN: 9781602730755 • 174 pages • $12.95 USD.

FAITH AFTER FAILURE
Reconnecting with Your Destiny
by Sandie Freed
ISBN: 9781602730557 • 208 pages • $13.95 USD.

WHY DO I DO THE THINGS I DO?
Understanding Personalities
by Dr. Darrell Parsons
ISBN: 9781602730199 • 132 pages • $10.95 USD.

RELEASE YOUR WORDS—IMPACT YOUR WORLD
by Dr. Darrell Parsons
ISBN: 9781602730007 • 140 pages • $9.95 USD.

EMERGING AS AN INNOVATIVE CHRISTIAN LEADER
12 Common Cores for Mobilizing Your Influence into the Future
by Dr. Darrell Parsons
ISBN: 9781602730656 • 228 pages • $14.95 USD.